Hunger

Hunger

POEMS by Lola Haskins

Story Line Press

Printed in the United States of America
Second edition

Book design by Richard Hendel

Library of Congress Cataloging-in-Publication Data

Haskins, Lola.
Hunger : poems / by Lola Haskins
p. cm.
ISBN 1-885266-35-9
I. Title.
PS3558.A7238H86 1996
811'.54—dc 20 96-30549
CIP

Contents

1 The Cow, 3
At Eighty, 4
The Dresser, 5
Freezer, 6
Extermination, 7
Flood, 8
The Fence, 9
Farm Wife, 10
Fishing, 11

2 Six Cairns for Mary, 15

3 The First Dinner Party—The Puzzles of the Meal, 23
Sweet Pea Embroidery in Rose and Heliotrope, 25
Of the Pleasures to Be Discovered in Books, 26
The Message of the Marriage Eve, 27
From "What Every Mother Should Know," 28
Gladys Suggests: Table Decorations for a Children's Party, 29
Coronation Embroidery, 30
Cookery: To Truss Small Birds, 31
How to Cut and Dry: Study of a Marriage, 32
Secrets of the Fur Trade, 33
Emeralds, 34
Fashion: How to Wear the Veil, 36

4 Exteriors: A Self-Guided Tour, 39

5 Elegy, 55
Infidel, 56
The Laws of Women, 57
On Passing Forty, 58
The Confrontation, 60
Acrylics, 61
Django, 62
A Confluence, 63
For Someone Considering Death, 64
Employment, 65

6 Xtofer and Elizabeth, 69

Acknowledgments

Some of the following poems have appeared in *Artful Dodge*, *Beloit Poetry Journal*, *Iowa Review*, *West Branch*, *Kestrel*, *New Virginia Review*, *Literary Review*, *California Quarterly*, *Missouri Review*, *Southwest Review*, *Midwest Quarterly*, *Southern Poetry Review*, *New England Review/Breadloaf Quarterly*, *Free Lunch*, *New York Quarterly*, *Georgia Review*, and *The Quarterly*.

Some also appeared in a limited-edition chapbook, *Across Her Broad Lap Something Wonderful* (State Street, 1989).

"Secrets of the Fur Trade," originally published in *Southwest Review*, was reprinted in *An Anthology of Magazine Verse and Yearbook of American Poetry* (Monitor Books, 1986).

"Fashion: How to Wear the Veil," originally published in *Iowa Review*, was reprinted in the 1989–90 edition of *An Anthology of Magazine Verse*.

"The First Dinner Party," originally published in *New Virginia Review*, was reprinted in *North of Wakulla* (Anhinga Press, 1990).

"Employment," originally published in *Beloit Poetry Journal*, was reprinted in *Polyphony: An Anthology of Florida Writers* (Panther Press, 1988).

"Six Cairns for Mary," selected by Maxine Kumin, won the 1988 *New England Review/Breadloaf Quarterly* narrative poetry prize.

I am grateful to the National Endowment for the Arts and the Florida Department of State for fellowships that supported the writing of some of these poems.

I

The Cow

Across her teeming back I strew
the poison cure.

Her tail turns still.
Soon she will be less thin.

But then again the black buzz,
the keen, upheaving bone.

And though I glove my hands,
I cannot help but breathe.

The sharp dust drifts,
each time deeper.

Don't do it, says my husband
who loves me, hearing

the hundred tiny cuts in
my throat. He does

not know how it feels
when the flies lift.

At Eighty

Perhaps the white with the sewn pearls,
as evenly strung as la-las. Then again,
maybe the dark blue, whose double buttons
gleam. Or the shawl for a change,
with its hooked-in holes and metal glints
running through the yarn.
                                        She stands
at the closet considering, as before
a late-night shop whose lit displays
look like nothing she ever owned.
And suddenly the choice matters terribly.
Her spotted hands begin to shake.
She is so afraid to be wrong.

The Dresser

For months no one has opened a drawer,
and inside
the tight-legged piles of underwear,
the rolled-together socks
that hate each other,
the shirts with their sleeves crossed
behind.

The oak grain has begun to swell
as a can will, whose red insides
have not been boiled past memory.
But these are only clothes.
Familiar things.
You dramatize.
                    No.
When they opened the dark mouth
of the cave
where the boy king slept in gold,
it was the simple air that screamed.

Freezer

Where eyes of round have forgotten
the quick knife that made them,
how the butcher stared against the light
as he leaned in his smeary apron
separating the parts of a carcass
that yet knew something of what he did—
that pain is gone. Where pale ears of corn
have forgotten how the wind used to dance
in their stalks, how bees would hum
in the close indigo. Where okra has frozen
in green fingers, which point
to the hearts of calves, grazing
in the rising grass of high summer,
not noticing that the egrets have begun
to leave, any more than they noticed
that their mothers had disappeared,
or that the moon was slow orange all week.
Only the freezer knows the truth—the end
of all such stories, after the ends
our mothers tell us as they smile on our beds
before they turn out the lights.
The last home of animals and gardens.
The dark. The cold. The waiting to be eaten.

Extermination

Flat to the bones of cupboards
like growths, behind the backs
of the bright cereals
and the soldiering cans of corn,
they stick their tight brown eggs.
And every night new roaches spill,
well forth into our household world.
And we wait for the lately hatched
to grow large and vulnerable.
We wait with spray cans, our thumbs
poised. We wait with one shoe
in the air, with a magazine rolled
tense. But their secret is that
they are so many, and that
they stay small. These do not die,
oozing yellow, in an almond haze.
So we set out poison, which
our children may eat after school,
or our dogs lick up. And we never
know. If they do die, it is
inside our walls, and in any case,
the thousands of tiny explosions,
the fallings-apart that happen
every day, do not matter. Turn on
a light in any dark, and see.

Flood

ALEXANDRIA, LOUISIANA

We have been four days on the second floor.
Four days since the brown water first
entered our home. It is two steps up,
and rising. Roberta holds my hand.
Her small fingers frighten, even in
my palm. Her braids pale around her face.
Hush, I tell her. Can you hear it?
And when she stills, we hear it.
Not with our ears
but with the parts of our bodies that know.
With our knees, with our low places.
Snakes, swimming.

The Fence

Oh how the dappled pony in the fog
gallops
as though he had eaten some beating thing
that strikes again and again the grass
and makes the wet sand fly.
How hungry he is.
How he rushes at the small jabs of wire
that scratch his flank
and catch the long hairs of his tail.
And away he gallops again, away,
across the bitten grass
and the sand showing through like a skull.

Farm Wife

She tends the red geraniums.
When their clustered eyes go dark,
she cuts them from their stems.
With her thumb she strokes the
furry leaves, not like common cloth
but the nap and shift of velvet
falling heavy over her hips,
the long slow dance
of Paris, in France.
The swoony glide of his knife
spreading butter.
Not the bread it takes her
all day to bake,
the coarse knead and punch,
but the rise,
the pale cheek of flour,
the dip and shimmer of the heat,
the arched backs of the hills
in their arms of sky.

Fishing

The sky has fallen asleep over
Malham Tarn,
over the bare fields strewn with sheep,
over the bitten moors
where long-armed men passed stones up the steep
to set them one by one in walls,
while their hairy daughters crouched,
pounding grain with other stones,
by Malham Tarn where even then
the stars went in the day.
Here is the pay for long patience.
At the end of your thin line, something gleams.

2 Six Cairns for Mary

Where the way over the moors turns

indistinct, heaps of stones serve to guide the walker

along the authorized path. No one alive remembers

who dragged them there.

Mary Attends a Ball
(1830)

Our candles shine plain as servant girls
before the moon, who wears the whitest dress
tonight. And all our India muslins,
and all our fine combs of filigree,
and all our long feathers
cannot rival how she flies.
And when the gentlemen roam the hall,
there comes a moment each forgets
the face or name of her he seeks.
And when memory returns, each thinks
himself wrong, it was someone else
he hunted, with such white fever.

Mary in Love

(1832)

If Mr. Peake stands booted on Ingleton Hill
and his big mare stamps beside him,
whose rein's a hard, dry catch in his palm,
and if the day spreads her fields,
yellow as head powders, at his feet,
and he is thinking which are ripe
and which not, then I would go to him
in the little wind which stirs his hair
and creeps among the folds of his stock
just before, all around,
the gold seed wisps begin to sway.

Mary, Waking

(1833)

Well, Mrs. Peake, he says. And smiles.
And when he's shut the door I rise
and put on my new dress, habit of wife,
grey as the feathers of doves
that peck at the bright litters
of corn someone strews for them
by the barn, whose stones weigh
heavier than hearts, more
than any man can heft alone.

His Breakfast Plate/The Litter of Mr. Peake

(1835)

Yellow smears upon a white ground.
Two greasy commas that remain of chops.
A knife thrust through the fork's tines.
And, over all, the scattered dots of crumbs
brushed from his hands as,
pig-shine on his lips, he turns to go.

Mary's Duties

(1836)

He is rid away to the tenant farms
and I take up my pen to list
the shakings-out and openings.
And my thin letters lean as sails
that, though driven, cannot arrive.

May the ninth, I write.
And: *Mrs. Ferguson.*
Unbutton the bedpillows
and plump them to the air.
Then: *Take the curtains down*
and with your broom unseat
the spiders' webs. Open

the windows and leave them
wide and here the thread trails
off, among the cottages
with their spring festoons of eggs
pricked with pins and blown,
fragile as the blacksmith's daughter
dreaming in the sun, who lifts
her skirts above her white knees.

I pull back behind a hedge.
Let her not meet me, with my dry pen.

The Very Reverend Charles Eaton
(1836)

Thursday last Mary Peake fell off her horse
and lit upon her ear.
She never spoke again, died in half an hour,
the child still in her.

This night the cat got to her corps,
et off bits of her nose and chin.
The rest took wind,
and is now in all our mouths.

3

The First Dinner Party—The Puzzles of the Meal

Among the forest of forks and spoons,
the young girl need not fear
who remembers that, as with life,
the proper meal progresses from outer,
to inner, settings. In conversation
with a partner, etiquette demands she not
assault his ear with girlish questions—
Don't you just adore Wagner? What are your
favorite plays?—until the gentleman
has satisfied his appetite, and then
she must speak only softly, and seldom,
on topics proper to her femininity.
When the finger bowl arrives, she must not
wash her grapes. If doubtful of the ways
of oranges, she must choose bananas.
When standing to leave the table, a lady
does not fold her napkin at her plate
but lets it fall, as too careful placement
implies an unseemly intention to return.

Oh Myrtle, do you think such rules
can truly bind the darker dinners of the heart?
As Charles is your brother, do you believe
I can win his favor laughing only gently,
speaking seldom, or might I, reaching across

the table, all the servants sent upstairs,
tell him quickly how I yearn? Might I wash
his grapes and hand them to him one by one?
If I, saying nothing, leave my napkin
folded by his plate, will he understand?

Sweet Pea Embroidery in Rose and Heliotrope

Let the needlewoman gather
a handful of the blossoms she loves most.
Now let her embroider in silks
the colors of that scent that entered
her room, its wilds of heliotrope, of rose.
But let her tell no one
how she left her bed, to stand
in her white nightgown among flowers.
And how the knowledge came to her
of what she can, and cannot, own.

Of the Pleasures to Be Discovered in Books

Sometimes in the long afternoons
as the light goes slowly slant into
the evening, I think I shall go mad.
I stand at the window with its stiff
velvet fringe. Behind me Aunt Jane is
cross-stitching my name in handkerchiefs.
The window looks about to speak.
What will it say? That no lady
calls without cards? That a lady
must yearn only for an upright man?
That I am no lady? Will it whisper scandal
against my name that daily grows in linens,
to live at the bottoms of drawers?
"You are unoccupied my dear," says Aunt Jane.
"Read to me awhile." I hate the color black.
Why must she wear shrouds? I open the book.
In the garden a moustached man is waiting.
His amused lips mock every word I say.

The Message of the Marriage Eve

The night before a lady is to be married, her attendants must search the folds of her wedding gown. If they find a spider, the bride will be lucky in her married life. If not, the opposite conclusion is thought to follow.

These folds ripple white as Arabian dunes.
Do you see, Martha? Imagine that some trip
is taking place within, like the journey
our Sarah prepares for tonight, that small
camels carry spices across the dip of her
waist, that a merchant awaits them and their
robed crew, satisfying his thirst at a rare
spring under palms. But Sarah shifts in
her sleep, the camels tumble to her bedchamber
floor, the merchant drowns, and we are left
alone, with only her wedding gown. We must
search it carefully. Should we miss the lady
spider, Sarah may one day hunger, her husband
lost, dead of fever in the India of her dreams,
her children thin and begging in the street.
We must not fail. Here in the folds of a sleeve
I think I saw . . . but no. Dawn is coming, Martha.
The sun is coming on like a horse through
the mist. What do you say? Shall we tell her
we saw no spider? Or shall we love her, and lie?

From "What Every Mother Should Know"

Oh, such a neglectful mother, Ann,
who left her child's first tooth, fallen,
to find its own rest, did not burn
the small bone as her mother told her,
did not fill it with salt, did not ask God
for a new one. And a hen, wandering in
the muddy yard, picked it up with a worm
and a wisp of hay. So Ann's poor child
grew a hen's tooth. And cackles leapt from
his mouth at odd moments, for the tooth
would not be still. And he dreams,
dear reader, no longer of his mother's milk
but of yellow, only yellow.

Gladys Suggests:
Table Decorations for a Children's Party

The snow is cotton wool, the little white teddies,
toys. Explorer dolls peer from matchbook tents
at a Union Jack, which floats briskly
on a pretend breeze. Two ships approach
the scene, across a mirror sound.

There is an ice fog. The ships do not
see the explorers. The explorers do not
see the ships, which slowly approach
the dark teeth of rocks under the snow.
A child bites into a marzipan doll.
An explorer is suddenly headless.
One ship's ribs crunch easily.
A chubby hand reaches for the other.
There can be no salvation before the blancmange.

Coronation Embroidery

Teach your daughters
the symbols of the Crown.
Tell them of the Cap of Maintenance
and the Cap of Estate.
Explain the presence of the fleur-de-lys.
In this way they may learn as babies
the great events
of which their little needles write,
and as women may come to understand
the places of their husbands and sons
among crimson threads knotted long ago
on the wrong side of the cloth.

Cookery: To Truss Small Birds

Thread wheatears, ruffs, or quails
on a long skewer, four or more together.
Pass the skewer through the wingtip
of each bird, and out its body
to the next. Secure with string.

See the little birds on their burning branch.
Their song sizzles from their beaks.
Their wings are tied.
How they would fly otherwise, on this ecstatic wind!

How to Cut and Dry: Study of a Marriage

With care the hedgerows can provide a thrifty wife
with winter bloom. Most prized of all is Honesty,
which must not be cut until quite dry, and should
then be hung upside down until its seedpods can
be removed, leaving only the white discs within.

It is so cold these days that my fingers stiffen,
reaching into the privet. This morning,
I cut my wrist on some brambles
but did not notice until the blood ran.
I have filled the house with winter's gifts.
In every closet something lies stiffening
between layers of old news. I have just
replaced the milkweed pods that used to stand
in a copper jug by the front door. They had
exploded, spilling seed across the entry. He
will not notice the fresh, green limbs of pine.

Secrets of the Fur Trade

Sable is for ladies of quality. The best
is Russian, with fine white hairs running
through the dark. They will try to sell you
poorer stuff, with badger hair glued in,
but you need not be fooled. Blow through
the fur. You will see the stiff lies,
which do not easily yield to a lady's
breath. Watch the merchant's eyes narrow,
as he sees you understand. If you'd asked
for rabbit, he'd have brought you cat.
Now tell him that you know, as well
as you know your own name—Esmee—
the greenish color of wet dyed fur,
the dark brown of the true. That he
must bring you from the back room,
where his wild son sits, ruining
his brown eyes over poems
(in which dim animals cross the snow
to be finished, one by one, for
the white moments of their coats),
the long fur of all their lives.
That you will purchase only this from him:
this rare darkness tipped with light,
to clothe your body in, against the many winters
a lady of quality must endure.

Emeralds

Through emerald lenses Nero sees the boy
whose fuzzy limbs have known his hand,
whose lips his own. In the dust
nets spin and miss. And now he nods.
The boy's green mouth begins to leak,
but what it asks is lost. The emperor
sheds his sight. The edges of the crowd
blur around his spoon-shaped eye.

*

The Syrian ambassador regards the emerald
carved with Cleopatra's face.
Green as watered fields her face in jewel,
cut from upper Egypt. Hard under his
fingers, her lips and hair. He asks
the assassin in, who'll bear her
Syria's gift. The men embrace.
The woman's face on the table casts
a green light on their own.

*

The emerald is the most ancient of jewels.
She is a fool who accepts pearls,
those emblems of the blind, before
the only worthy gift: a glitter eye
of green, bright as her body under her clothes,
sudden as the stare of a cat
to a small animal at the end of its life.

Fashion: How to Wear the Veil

With black jet stars artfully placed
above a bare chin. This is the way
of the flirt. With the veil caught
back, to hang unhampered to the wearer's
waist. This is the way of the free
American, of the summer girl.
Then, there is the decorous way,
the understatement from a hat.
This is the way of the well bred.

And finally, there is the nun,
who goes differently veiled, morning
and afternoon. This is the way of
the truly passionate, the way of
the woman who stands in the wind
at the needle's shiny point, her
face covered, who does not look down.

4 Exteriors: A Self-Guided Tour

ROOM I (Mexico, oils 1969–71)

Avenida

Here is the street, the way the heat
settles in the dust.
If it rained now, the first surge
would be lost, would puddle, then
hurry up and dry as though it never came,
the way the bride does not remember
her wedding night, how her new man
unzipped black legs. She has forgotten
the strange dripping weight
like the oppression of withheld rain.
She looks out the window.
                                        One thin child
hops in the avenue. Over a dust line
into a little cloud, and back again.
He keeps his arms tucked to his sides,
and she thinks of the thousands
of small singers at home, jittering among
the crowded leaves.
                                They came to the capital
for Juan's work. All day he hammers copper
into suns. When he comes from the market,
the din comes too, clings to the folds
of his shirt, lingers in his fine

cheek hair. She turns warm tortillas
into a basket. He pulls her around.
There is a hint of metal on his tongue
as though he had licked money.
                                                            You can
just see her face at the edge of the third
window. She has hung a blanket over the hole
to keep out the dust. I never intended
to paint her. I wanted only the street,
the child with the dry mouth.
I meant all the windows to be dark.

Mercado

The blank sockets of devilfish,
hung drying to the light, watch me
down the aisles of heavy papayas
like full breasts, follow me into
the tight hearts of onions, into
the mouths of ollas, with their damp
clay air. I rub them gone.
My view clears to the stripes
of a serape, braids itself down
the back of an old woman, who squats
behind red pots which nobody buys.
Her eyes, black as rain fallen
in a cenote, meet my eyes. My skin
rises. My brushes lift in their box.
I take her home, carry her, wrinkled
and light, over my threshold.
I buy all the red pots.

Fábrica

I choose a brush to make the thick
streak of the sun behind the factory.
Juan is leaving. I steal the jacket
from his shoulders, and its umber
migrates to the smokestack
and fades into the air.
                                        Pepe pays
no attention. He has a woman
to get to who wears a print dress
and high heels, and can cook arroz
like no one in this world.
He is the one I want.
I have put on his face
what he feels, entering her door.

Viuda

This is the bus station.
This is the viuda who waits in line.
She wears black. She wears thick shoes.
I have frozen her with ten counted pesos
under the grill of the ticket window.
In her purse, which she has set down,
is a pension card, a *tarjeta* from her
soldier son in Mazatlán, and her mud hut
with its magnificent marriage bed,
its Virgin, and its eight white hens,
closed in because she fears dogs.
Under the bed are three bloodstained eggs.
She will find them tonight.

Untitled

Lately I have noticed a change
of palette. There are oranges
which are brighter than life,
hansas and chromes seasoned
like tourists' toys. There is
a crimson which has grown too bold,
demands not to be mixed.

I can
no longer paint what hangs in shadow.
Is it this bright air, blinding me of
boyhood Gloucestershire? Or is it that
I paint now with closed eyes, paint
what I see rubbing the lids,
gay fireworks even a hungry child
can own? How deep can they fly
into the night before they fall,
little rainy sparks, and the sky afterwards,
darker than it was?

ROOM 2 (Mexico, watercolors 1972–73)

Sky, Mazatlán

I am learning to say no
when a beggar pulls at my trouser leg
with his three-fingered hand.
I am learning to hold my own brushes,
and sometimes I come home from painting
and my fingers do not ache at all.
There is the illusion of ease
these days in the way the sky opens
its white breasts of cloud,
and sometimes I even think I could
paint them, before they change
into something else.

View of Dzibichaltún

I make my softest brushes from the hairs
of my own head. Only these understand
to wash so faintly
that the shadow hand which cups
a cheek can be rendered private,
safe from those who look,
then go.
            There is a sky in my
View of Dzibichaltún that recalls
the slow violet light of bruises.
For this and for the river, I used
such brushes. They sold none there,
and my case held nothing so lost.
So I tied my own pulled hairs
and from their tips water began
to flow over my stippled paper,
burying the false starts underneath,
the jumbled heads, the botched bones,
heaped so high the ferry sometimes
scrapes, and the boatman swears to
the Virgin between rotting teeth
until his pole catches deeper,
and his flat boat slides on.
                                        She
was not with me then. I sat alone
on the damp grass, finishing the water,
beginning to wash in the sky.

And I put into the picture what
I did not paint, the fading pastel
houses of the rich, who do not come
from Veracruz anymore; the unglazed
pots of the poor, who sling their
hammocks in the big rooms; the bird eyes
of the old woman who killed
her one chicken for a guest, then
gummed the claws, refusing more,
while he, I, ate all the rest.
                                        You say
these are not there? She found them.
She looked into the river,
then turned silent, staring across
the London dark, through the rain.

ROOM 3 (London, various media 1974–79)

Night Cove (watercolor)

I scrape the thin line
off a shrimp's back
and clean my knife on paper
which, opened, explodes with
star-bursts of entrails.
There is a pile of heads and shells.
There is a heap of boneless embryos.
Shrimp curl inwards, like her asleep.
She is so pale the veins shine
in her breasts. Her hair spreads
faint strands, like feelers, over
the pillow. Her lids are ghost eyes,
like the eyes of cave fish
who do not need light. I think
she would gleam in the moon
like something swimming.
                                        I have
painted her like this. She is
the white glow that hovers under
the little boat in the night cove
where a father has taken his son
to fish, these two who go
so that the father can touch
the boy's shoulder in a way

he cannot, unless they are alone,
and the boy can understand
how he is loved. The moon
is making them a path over the
dark water. She is the pale streak
they do not see, finning past
their unbaited hooks as a woman
shifts in sleep, with this grace.

Nude (pencil)

She leans nude into the Chelsea night.
There are no stars or moon,
only the wet splash of street lamps
and the glowing bars of zebra crossings.
I have put out the lights.
I am drawing her by feel, the arch
of one leg as she settles into
the window seat, like a white neck rising
from the Ness. Earlier, we tried
another kind of love. We thrashed
and surged in the sheets. I could not
reach her. She turned away,
the sad damp trailing along
her thighs.
                    I am drawing her in the
dark, because if I see what my hand
is making, I will never finish.
I will never again lie all night
by the lake, staring into its
black waters with such craving.

Piece of Man, with Park (oil)

She sets out plates,
the eternal bubble and squeak,
a sludgy mass that catches, going
down. Behind me canvases lean,
so many I cannot shift my chair.
Dull parks, great looming trees,
dog litter, wrappers, leftovers
from other hungers. The people
are beginning to disappear. In the last
there is only a man's arm. I thought
he fell, struck with a pain in
his chest which tightened under his
tatty coat until his walk became a lie.
She smiles across the table. I tell her
a bit of kale is caught in her teeth.
She scrapes at it. It is still there.
It has left the canvas,
this dark and creeping green.

ROOM 4 (New York, oils 1980–)

I am working on a new series: *Gold*
on Gold. Each, over an old canvas,
erases what was. I never thought
gold so subtle: the bit of dull at
the edge of an eye, a moneyed leaf,
worthy of the gleam heart of Angelico.
The first depicts my bald head
on a serving tray. A dark pool, the dim
of treasure under water, spreads from
the chin. My second is a steamer trunk.
What is inside does not matter. I wanted
the patina of its surface, curved gently
as a woman's cheek, with its fingerprints
too smudged to be identified.
I am starting the third. It is the moment
leaves catch wind, just before
the odd yellow light breaks. My pausing brush
bleeds onto the floor. Of a sudden,
the ochre sky swirls around me. Whole trees
twist from their roots. And rise.

5

Elegy

FOR HARRY HUMES

Red-shouldered at four o'clock
swings binoculars to the right
over the breast of the ridge
to zoom the lone bird
that screams, passing the cold
rocks of Hawk Mountain.
And a chill seeps into the pockets
of the watchers, to climb,
as the light fails, higher.
You unscrew the wine. We drink
from the same skin and when
the call comes, *Sharpies at eleven*,
we swing our eyes south.
This is what we came for, Harry.
To become, only for a moment,
what we dreamed we were as children.
Something wild, flying away.

Infidel

The brittle wing in the salad.
The fuzzy cocoon, floating
in the cola bottle.
The hard brown kernels
in the rice that are
not rice. In your drawer,
her letters.

I have noticed you are balding.
I have noticed the strain
at your buttons.
Why should I say anything?
Only that there are
too many stars tonight.
Such crowded shine.
Like her,
with all Woolworth's at her throat.

The Laws of Women

The blood mouse hangs by her tail
and, dropped, whirls down.
What returns is so clear
you could drink it.
Children sometimes do. And dogs.
But not us. We have rules
for what we drink.
And when we wake in the barking night,
we have learned
to flush, not thinking,
what has seeped most darkly from ourselves.

On Passing Forty

You with your mesmerizing eyes,
you holding a daubed cracker
between first finger and thumb,
so absurd in your huge foreign hands.
You the priest, with your obscene thoughts.
The gold water in your glass disappears,
leaving ice. And you look up.
I will not go with you.
I am happy. I have decided
my life, and it does not take place
in rooms like this.
                                        In certain years
marriage darkens in my throat.
In certain years I am aware
of the way white hairs fall
around my face, killing the black ones
underneath. I smile too much,
and the skin deepens around my mouth.
At times like these, you appear.
In the street you pause to buy
a paper, and your eyes travel
my body, leaving it throbbing,
bright and pulpy as a heart.

At a party, as now, you single me,
and my fingertips shiver as though
I'd run them around your white collar,
pulled it wide, set my lips to your
bare skin. I am happy, I say.
The wind gathers your black cape,
and sends it flying.

The Confrontation

The air's dead weight,
like breasts before the blood
breaks, like grapes in pain
about to fall.

And dark, like the silence
between two people
when one has just said
the true, hard, angry thing.

Then suddenly,
lightning splits the oak
and nothing
will bring it back.

Not any word.
Not concrete poured too late
into the tree's heart.
Not all this rain.

Acrylics

From the primary colors, you've learned
to make your own. Little one, who caps
invented mountains with enthusiastic snow,
small painter who lives in flat country . . .

I will buy you a fan brush with real camel hair.
Then your branches can float
and your shadows travel the lakes upside down.
I could take you to mountains,
show you how the earth's knees buckled,
like a body jackknifing under pressure.
But you know about that. You are twelve.
What you have to learn comes soon:
how thin the air is in high places,
how your fingers can go numb at the tips,
that it is possible to lose a hand.
It will come to you. How to paint the cold.

Django

In the middle of the night he arrives
with his pillow. He climbs between us
and slowly his shivers die.
                                        He heard
the leaves move in the yard, a step
at a time.
                This is what we live for,
you and I. This private moment when
he settles into our breathing, and
we are three birds on one dark swell,
a lifetime from any land we knew.

A Confluence

The clear Ichitucknee fingers into
the dark red Santa Fe,
which carries purity and great cold
downstream
until it is lost in murk of sun
where wrist-thick moccasins ess along
and alligators surface, then disappear,
or drag their bellies up the muddy shore.
We have forgotten who we were, young
and eager, kissing through the telephone.
The Suwannee is in no hurry,
has rocked all the humming afternoon.
Now she takes two yarns from a basket
at her side, and with long, white needles
begins to knit. The low sun glints
on the tips of her flying. Across her
broad lap, something wonderful begins.

For Someone Considering Death

I told you.
Life is one big Hanon
up and down the piano,
five fingers skipping over each other
in every conceivable way,
two hands getting stronger.

And sure,
the notes are the same for everyone,
but you can choose to whisper or shout,
to fade or grow.
And haven't you noticed that some people's hands sing
but others are midwestern on the keys,
each crescendo a secretarial swell.

Think about this.
How can you dream to play the *Pathétique*,
how can the moment come to truly look
into someone's eyes
and say, *The hell with everything, I love you*,
when you haven't done your time,
hour after hour, year after year,
in that small, closed room.

Employment

Every day I suck a little marrow.
I can feel my bones hollowing.
Sometimes the empty spaces ache
like a limb that isn't there.
Sometimes the air gets in
and I can't control the tune
it sings. I am doing the best
I can. I know the fine hairs
that grow along my arms are not
feathers yet. But I never sleep
without saying the prayer,
never forget, even in dreams,
what I am to be. And I practice,
lifting the right muscles,
doing wind sprints, everything
you say, understanding
all this time that my pay
can be no more than you own.
Which is nothing more than
my light self, surging in
the air, then going down.

6 Xtofer and Elizabeth

1712

He comes to the house and asks,
How do ye? then looks out the window
at the fine clouds or the rainy weather,
then again at me as though I would answer
for it all. And then he smiles.
Then Father's from his walk, sets his thumbstick
in the stand, takes Xtofer's arm
and off they go, to the deep seats where men
discuss together, Father and his solicitor,
this very Christian lawyer.
And I, wondering what he means.

Times at night, when the coals
are red eyes in the ash
and the chambermaid is gone away,
I see Grandmother
when she was Jennet the child,
leaning on the stone sill
in the moon, her hair loosed yellow,
thinking for the first time
how very many stars there be.

1715

TO X

From my window I watch your nagg
being led to grass, her withers
smooth stones in the wavery light.
Below stairs a goose hisses through
her pricked skin. On a cloth
a roll of brawn awaits
the first clean slice to fall.
And you and father talk weather,
the odd flood that swept a
carriage house down the Ayr, the
man who shouldered up the roof beam
while his wife and child
crawled out between his legs.
Then wind crushed the thatch,
and splintered his slow bones.
Your words seep darkly through the floor.

1715

They have held the Assize of Bread
at Leeds, and set new rates
for wheaten loaves which enrage
the millers, says Xtofer,
and he and Father go on anent
the wet year, and the winnowing
of hay to fatten the barns
by Michaelmas if the stacks
be not rotten from beneath.
They do not glance at me,
and for my part I am sensible only
of the stuff that lies against
my skin. The chance brush of
petticoat along my unclothed leg
must drive me wild, I think,
as our puss went that found
a small green herb, which he
rubbed at and purred deeper
in his throat than ever
I heard him do before. Then
he thought to bite its heart.
And went leaping through the grounds.
I can still conjure him, rolling
on the grass, huge dragon wings
ashiver in his mouth.

1716

TO X

The maids have carried off the mutton
and pyes and we three nest in the parlour,
you and Father in your Virginia cloud, I
pricking out a pansy scheme, then beginning
to stitch it in. And here's sweet discussion
of some small matter, say the arrival of
a Doctor of Teeth in Bingley Tuesday last.

And at this moment I am aware that my waist
presses against my gown. And I watch
your dear face in candlelight and consider
the story I'll tell when the bedcurtains
are drawn tonight.
                                        I have seen the grass
moving in just such a slight way
before the grouse break free, whose wings
beat high and sound like rain. I have
not caused their flight, but only
point it out. Think upon it if you will.
I am, dear Cedar, your most humble
and creeping bramble, Elizabeth.

1716

As Xtofer in black awaits where I come
in russet silk, we two fall together
into this high mystery, as one bird folds
its wings and dives. And Mother's eyes
discolour in their frame. What this means
I cannot think, for my hand is safe
inside the solicitor's, new counsel
and judge of this house, with its wedding
tables of peacock and swan and egret and
venison and lamb. And man and wife, we turn
at last from deserted planks heaped tall
with bitten thighs, and ribs with their tufts
of meat not quite persuaded from bone.
And joined we mount the stairs,
in the center of the case
where the stone dips, worn and smooth.

1720

Elizabeth Danby I am, who was Wren,
and once more low with child.
She will be Jennet if she lives.
Never did I hear her sisters cry,
but they lay ivoried in their white gowns.
When the last was dead, he could not wait
the gander moon, but entered early,
with drawn tool. And shining eyes
like night sonnes. And now he writes
his name for two:
Xtofer.

1723

The comfort is damp to the skin,
red satin like cold stone.
And I know, Xtofer, where you lye
though you think me a fool
who believes your mincing pleadings,
your words fine as dark thread
wet with her lips.
                                        I dreamt
you rode the stang, that they stuffed
you full of straw and stitched you up
and painted you crooked, catchpaper
varlet that snatches more than
your own, and on a stick you went
who were so dear to me, between
Cuddy the butcher, and Tom who
sells ale. And the smelly crowds
jeered you out and dogs ran after.
I wake to rain, and chill unseasonable,
and damp's frog mouth pressed to my bone.
In the next room you are dressing,
fumble-fingers for the dark.
Outside stirs restless your stoned mare.
You cannot wait till morning, to go to her.

1724

Jennet stirs in so frail sleep.
I stroke her three years' curls,
more pale than they seem by day.
I hear he rode from the Angel
to the Two-Necked Swan. He was
not alone, and will he return
I know no more than I know
of that place where kings' flesh
be venison and the true angels
weep and sing. I will stay
all night by her,
only to see her eyelids flutter.

Dearest Jennet, take my life,
this broken odd rhapsody of scraps,
and know the truth of love:
that no matter where you hide,
chyld or woman, the moon and stars
will cross the dark to find you.

Other Books by Lola Haskins

Extranjera
(forthcoming)
Story Line Press, 1997

Visions of Florida
University Press of Florida, 1994

Hunger
University of Iowa Press, 1993
Second Edition, Story Line Press, 1996

Forty-Four Ambitions for the Piano
University Presses of Florida, 1990
Second Edition, Betony Press (FL), 1994

Across Her Broad Lap Something Wonderful
State Street Press (NY), 1989

Castings
Countryman Press (VT), 1984
Second Edition, Betony Press (FL), 1991

Planting the Children
University Presses of Florida, 1983

The Iowa Poetry Prize Winners

1987
Elton Glaser, *Tropical Depressions*
Michael Pettit, *Cardinal Points*

1988
Bill Knott, *Outremer*
Mary Ruefle, *The Adamant*

1989
Conrad Hilberry, *Sorting the Smoke*
Terese Svoboda, *Laughing Africa*

The Edwin Ford Piper Poetry Award Winners

1990
Philip Dacey, *Night Shift at the Crucifix Factory*
Lynda Hull, *Star Ledger*

1991
Greg Pape, *Sunflower Facing the Sun*
Walter Pavlich, *Running near the End of the World*

1992
Lola Haskins, *Hunger*
Katherine Soniat, *A Shared Life*